A Tiny Book *of* Romance

Steve Silberberg

Callipygian Ventures, Inc.
Hull, MA
USA

This legal disclaimer makes it seem like I'm an overbearing jerk, but all
it takes is one sleazy yahoo with a bankroll and a penchant for theft, and
the 3 hours I spent thinking up ideas for this book goes down the drain.

For information write to [*like anyone who's not a credit card company sends
U.S. mail*] Callipygian Ventures, Inc., 159 Nantasket Rd, Hull, MA 02045.
617-946-3566 [*that's 617-WIN ELMO*]

2nd Edition

ISBN: 0-9700815-8-8

Library of Congress Control Number: 2003090301

Cover & Book Design
Tina Aitala Engblom

Edited by
Leatrice Spevack

THIS BOOK IS DEDICATED TO MY LATE FATHER AND MY HERO, ARTHUR SILBERBERG, WHO TAUGHT INTEGRITY BY EXAMPLE.

I would like to take this opportunity to thank my mother, Noa Miller. Without her (and chemicals) life itself would be impossible.

Thanks to Carrie, Murray, and Dave, who read and commented on less polished [*if that were possible*] versions of the book, as well as Laura Ford who helped with early design efforts.

Finally, I'd like to thank Laura Conklin-Raymond for her diligent work in editing the first version.

By the way, if books were afforded the same latitude as movies, I could periodically splatter more acknowledgements throughout the first 30 pages of this book without having you think I'm a complete dolt.

Table of
Contents

Preface . . . . *ix*

Introduction 1

    What is Romance? 1

1. The Approach 5

    The Martial Arts Approach 6

    The Tab Stand 7

    Welcome to College 8

    Hi Citizen! 9

    Duct Tape is Better Than Either 10

    Missing Your Stop 11

    Bus Poetry 12

    Profiles Dating Service 13

    First Day of Work 14

    Patsy 15

    Do You Want Fries With That? 17

2. Personal Ads (That don't work) 19

3. Personal Ads (That work) 23

4. Romantic Dates (I've Had) 27

    The Laundromat 28

    Apple Picking 30

    Barry Manilow 31

    The Airport Game 32

    Airplane Dinner Party 33

The TRAAM 34

Clothes Shopping 36

Tree Climbing 38

Tree Climbing with a Surprise 39

Boo! 40

We Deliver For You 41

We'll Kiss For Food 42

5. Romantic Dates (I want to have) 45

Discovery Zone 46

Pet Birthday 47

Advanced Laundromat 48

Santa Trifecta 49

WWW 50

Restaurant in the Woods 52

E-Food 53

Flip a Coin Hike 54

Anyone Can Be on TV 55

Reverse Halloween 56

Sousa Picnic 57

6. Romance Every Day 59

7. Romance After Marriage 65

8. Romantic Gifts 67

9. Miscellaneous 71

Nicknames 71

The Dancing Game 72

The Value of a Date 74

Getting There 75

First Kiss 76

Homemade Greeting Cards 77

The Earring 79

The Earring, Part II 80

I'm Sorry 81

Planting Cabbage 83

Markar K. Nahabidian 84

Pizza Guy 85

10. Five Guys You'll Always Lose Out To 87

The Fast Car Guy 88

The Rich Guy 89

The Actor 90

The Italian Guy 91

The Bad Boy 93

Conclusion 95

Zusammenfassung 96

Is This Book Fiction? 97

Preface

The back cover of this book shows a picture that was taken on a recent date in an apple orchard. Taking Denise apple picking was romantic, no doubt about it.

A romantic man will take a woman apple picking. If this is you, congratulations. You are a romantic man. You have differentiated yourself from most other men in the pack. But that's not really the point here.

While apple picking is romantic, the real romantic gesture is going one step further and putting Denise's face on the cover of my book. See, the main point of this book isn't to educate, entertain, or amuse. It's all about doing something romantic for my girlfriend.

And going that extra mile is precisely the type of thing that will make you a romantic man.

Another Book on Romance?

Why do you care what I think about romance? You don't.

I am by no means some expert on romance. Like most computer geeks, I've never really been all that popular with women.

However, I figured that writing a book might make me more interesting to them. Unfortunately, the book that I wrote on C++ programming failed to attract any women [*next time I'm putting Fabio on the cover*]. So here's a book on romance instead.

Introduction

What is Romance?

TO HEAR MOVIES TELL IT, romance is all about a quiet candlelight dinner. A fire is burning in the fireplace and flowers are on the table. Soft music is playing in the background. You're dressed seductively and you share a bottle of wine.

That *is* romantic...

...maybe the first 17 times or so.

But romance, like fitness, is a lifestyle, not an event. Being romantic is something you do every day, not just on her birthday, or New Year's Eve, or your anniversary.

So what exactly does romance entail? Let's begin with the 6 Golden Rules of Romance.

[*Note: These are actually 6 characteristics, not rules. But saying "rules" makes it sound like you can be romantic if you just follow the recipe.*]

The **6** Golden Rules of Romance

1 *Romance is spontaneous.* It happens during a thunderstorm, or while taking out the trash, or on the anniversary of the invention of polyester.

> **2** *Romance is platonic.* The best romance occurs in the mind. Like love, romance is a cerebral manifestation of emotions that are not necessarily physical. Almost everything you will read about in this book is fairly innocent, and may bring you back to a time when romance was all you knew.

3 *Romance is unconventional.* Conventional means boring. Be a little creative. While sending her a greeting card on her birthday is somewhat romantic, thousands of guys have probably done this [*if she's Madonna, anyway*]. Instead, e-mail The White House and have them send her a birthday card on behalf of the President. That is very romantic.

Most people are really very creative. And although they may have anesthetized their originality with too much TV, a romantic man won't make that mistake.

> **4** *Romance has nothing to do with money.* Try this experiment. On your first date, take a dollar you receive in change and put it aside in a safe place [*which you probably already do if you're as cheap as me*]. Frame it, write her a short love note and put it aside.
>
> Exactly six months later, take a $50 bill and some pocket change, frame it and write her another short love note. Give them both to her. Which gift do you think she'll tell her friends about? [*Answer: Neither. Try this with $10,000 instead.*] Could it be that sentimentality is more romantic than cash?

5 *Romance is public.* While romance is typically private, as in the candle-light dinner scenario, it should also include the public declaration of love. Although this aspect of romance is often neglected, it can be a source of pure joy and magic in a relationship.

Many men don't even like to hold hands in public. It's as if it indicates some twisted denial of their machismo. If this is you, get over it. Maybe this works in front of your big important friends at the country club, but it's not going to bring romance to your life.

6 *Romance is risky.* Take a chance by risking personal embar-rassment. Acting silly or outrageous in front of the world to show someone you care is romantic. Courtship is all about risk. So why stop taking risks once you're in a relationship? Women appreciate daring men.

Never be afraid to embarrass yourself. Why worry about being judged harshly by nonromantic onlookers? You experi-ence embarrassment when you have the hubris to think people are actually looking at you or care about what you do. They don't. They are too self-absorbed.

{ So be romantic. All it takes is a little creativity, thought, and sometimes a bit of courage on your part. If you heed all the advice mentioned in this book to the letter, I guarantee that you will become known as a romantic man. [*You will also become known as a lemming-like automaton that follows directions out of a book without critically adjudging the merit of the advice.*]

1.
The
Approach

HOW DO YOU APPROACH A WOMAN? It's a time-honored question. Women typically feel most comfortable being approached in socially acceptable situations, such as at a party or a club. [*These situations tend to favor men who shop at the stores with the largest advertising budget*].

While this is understandable, you should realize that almost every situation is an opportunity to meet someone, whether it's the grocery store, a restaurant, or the park [*people don't actually go to parks anymore because it typically means walking is involved, but everyone's used to seeing them in this kind of list*]. You just have to make your approach in a non-threatening, yet somehow captivating manner.

And believe it or not, just walking up and saying, "hi" is often non-threatening and captivating enough to make a connection. [*If you're a dark haired 6'2" bodybuilder with steely blue eyes, "Hi" is optional*].

The Martial Arts Approach

It worked! After all, it's difficult to ignore a running Kung-Fu drop kick. Especially as someone sails over your beach blanket with serious hang time.

Around 1981, Danny Boy, Gomez, and I, three unremarkable MIT nerds, were walking down the Esplanade in Boston when we spied the two pretty Boston University women sunbathing. We stopped to check them out and were soon lamenting our inability to approach them (or any women for that matter).

Being young and not very romantic, I figured "chicks dig martial arts". I was wrong of course, but the drop kick did break the ice. And although the women initially reacted with total disdain, both Danny Boy and Gomez had gotten a phone number from each woman within 30 minutes.

Romance Factor: Low. But hey, it was college and it did meet with moderate success (especially if you happened to be Danny Boy or Gomez).

Lesson: Be different. Be dramatic. Male peacocks are dramatic. It piques interest and overcomes the tentative awkwardness of a subtler, more conventional approach. Convention, while cozy and reassuring, is dull, dull, dull. You're a romantic man, not a corporation [*or a peacock*].

The Tab Stand

Before Diet Coke the stereotypical Boston University woman used to drink a lot of Tab. At my friend Woddman's suggestion, I set up a "Tab Stand" to meet unsuspecting Tab drinkers (translation: women).

We pulled an old couch and serving table out to one of the streets on campus and set up. I purchased some plastic screw together champagne glasses, ice, and a lot of Tab and made a sign that said, "Free Tab". Although we offered free Tab to people all afternoon, we were ultimately unable to meet many women [*and the few we met didn't always need the extra calorie*].

This early and failed attempt at being romantic taught me that the phrase "Free Tab" isn't the one that makes a woman's heart melt. [*Many years later I was to find out that "Free trip on my boat" is*].

Romance Factor: Low. While fun, the Tab Stand turned out to be a really poor way to meet women. Even though not one man stopped for free Tab, few of the actual customers engaged us in any kind of flirtatious repartee.

Lesson: There is an unwritten hierarchy of romantic beverages. Champagne is romantic. Tab isn't, even if served in a champagne glass. Hot chocolate with marshmallows? Romantic. Prune juice? Not until you're 80.

While you may conclude that only intoxicants are romantic [*because they're good for getting women to compromise their principles, which is nice if that's your goal instead of lasting intimacy*], how do you explain the fact that wine is very romantic but beer isn't? I can't. I don't understand why anyone thinks that getting plastered is romantic at all.

Dallas, TX has a very elite clique known as the "Margarita Society". It sounds very mysterious and romantic doesn't it? But for some unknown reason, society members who are proud of their affiliation wouldn't be caught dead joining the "Malt Liquor Society".

Welcome to College

Timing can be important in an approach. I just happened to be walking out of my residence as Karen's father said goodbye to her, shut his car door, and pulled off. Timing was of the essence. Within split seconds, I greeted her with an exuberant "Welcome to College!" We spoke for a while and eventually became good friends.

We might have actually dated if Hondo hadn't yelled out the window of the standing room only party at Raleigh House, "Debbie is in here looking for you". But he did and we didn't.

Romance Factor: Moderate. In some convoluted way, there is something romantic about letting a woman know that she's desirable in her first instant of a life transition. There really is something to love at first sight. Once you hesitate, the moment is lost forever. This would be very romantic at someone's first day of work, if it weren't so completely inappropriate.

Lesson: "Welcome to College" won't work at clubs and bars because the approach is expected, you don't know if the object of your affection is going through a life transition, and bars and clubs are for beautiful people [*they think so*] who socialize best when their insipid banter is shrouded by ear piercing music.

Hi Citizen!

When in doubt, emulate super heroes. My buddy Tom, who I met at Math Camp [*Translation: Never had a date*], noted how Spiderman always categorized people he didn't know as "Citizens", using the catch phrase "Hi Citizen" as a greeting.

Well if it's good enough for Spiderman, it's good enough for me.

I was walking down the street one day getting to know Dimitri during his first week as a freshman. Using all the charm and romance that I had learned from Spiderman, I approached an unsuspecting female pedestrian with the opening line "Hi Pedestrian". It could have been "Hi Citizen" or "Hi Taxpayer" or something similar. That much is lost to history.

We sidled up beside her, seamlessly integrating our path with hers. Within 15 minutes we had quite unintentionally walked her home. This may sound scary, but it happened during a more innocent time. At her door, I got her phone number. The usually outspoken Dimitri never even uttered a word.

Although this encounter was promising, I never did call her, even though she wasn't an automatic disqualification. In not calling, I broke the cardinal rule of romance.

$\Big\{$ *Cardinal Rule of Romance*:
If you say you're going to call, CALL.

If you break this rule, you are a moron. It's incredibly rude to ask for a number and never call. If you want to be a romantic man, call just to say it was nice to meet her, even if you've decided you aren't really interested in her after all [*Translation: Disgusting pig*]. If you feel uncomfortable doing this, don't ask for her number you stupid dolt! It's called integrity.

Romance Factor: Low, unless you happen to be a Superhero.

Lesson: I'm a moron.

Duct Tape is Better Than Either

Occasionally, absurd or non-traditional opening lines can be romantic. Amy was in her room in a building in which we both lived, unaware that in a single moment, her life was going to change permanently. Although I had never met Amy, I was good friends with her sister Lina Bina.

Barging in through her open door, I queried, "Do you prefer electrical tape or masking tape?" Without missing a beat, I believe she replied, "masking tape". I left.

Sometimes, but not usually, an approach of this sort can be the beginning of a nice relationship. And although this portentous conversation transpired 18 years ago, Amy now sits in the office right next to me doing important mission critical work for our company while I sit here wasting company money writing about masking tape.

Romance Factor: Low. Most women hate nontraditional approaches that aren't TV tested. This is because it's difficult to immediately discern whether an absurd opening line comes from a romantic man or a nutcase.

Lesson: Thinking women [*Most guys don't want thinking women. It's too threatening for them*] are completely jaded by the same old questions.
— What's your name?
— Where do you live?
— What do you do? [*Men usually don't care about what you do, even if they're married to you*]
— Hot weather we've been having, huh?
Some women actually appreciate being asked something different.
— What's the best bargain you got recently?
— What city would you most like to visit and why?
   (This could lead her to think you might whisk
   her off on a vacation there [*You won't, of course*])
— What's the best gift you ever got from a boyfriend? This question
   reveals a lot about her past and also shows you care about her
   likes and tastes.
— How many teeth would you have to lose before you decided
   to pull them all and get dentures? [*Don't ask this in Arkansas*].

Missing Your Stop

About the most romantic thing you can do on a bus (or subway, or commuter rail or other public transportation including elevators) is to miss your stop for someone.

I once rode a Tri-Met bus all the way to the end of the line in Tualatin, OR to keep a compelling conversation going with a woman [*Translation: nice legs!*]. As we got to the last stop, I stood up to my fear of rejection and asked her out.

She was married! Not only did I lose the girl and miss my stop, I had to pay an extra sixty cents to get back home. But this experience was not without its lessons.

Later that summer, a woman named Katie missed her stop for me. From my earlier experience I knew that yes, she would be mine. We actually did go out on a date together, but I moved away from Oregon a few days after our only date.

Lesson: Check the ring finger before missing your stop.

Romance Factor: Pretty good. But not as good as…

Bus Poetry

[*Note to Whitey: Two consecutive chapters about busses means it's time to put this book down and pick up something more relevant to your life, like People Magazine.*]

Writing poetry is the most romantic thing you can do on a bus [*Or train, or commuter rail or other public transportation, but **not** on an elevator. That would be retarded.*] Writing poetry makes you seem like you're a passionate artiste.

Of course, if you actually are a poet, you probably don't have enough money to ride a bus. And although conventional wisdom says you're already reasonably romantic and don't need this chapter, you're also probably bitter, disenfranchised and use poetry cathartically to work out your intense personal pain.

Anyway, if you're not a poet, that's OK. Just write whatever you're thinking about [*except sports or your mother*]. If your poems end up being crappy stink pickles, don't worry; you'll never have to share them. But it's worth a shot. Even bad poetry has inherent romantic value.

Writing poetry has never really panned out as a romantic way of meeting anyone for me, but it may for you. It has certainly fascinated some of my fellow riders who considered me "sensitive", if that's a good thing. If nothing else, sensitive guys certainly save a lot of money on batteries and leather goods.

I don't know if bus poetry will work for you, but if it doesn't, at least you will have examined some of your inner feelings, like Oprah indoctrinates women to do. [*Women say they want you to express your inner feelings but at the same time don't want to be dating a wimp. One of many no-win situations you'll face as a romantic man.*]

Romance Factor: Low. It would be high if it weren't for the fact that you're on public transportation.

Lesson: If you somehow manage to impress a woman with poetry, she will probably expect you to treat her to sappy movies like "The Joy Luck Club" for the rest of your life.

Profiles Dating Service

I used to belong to a Jewish Dating Service called Profiles. When you join Profiles, you are instructed to fill out a three-page questionnaire [*Women want 10 pages, men only need a photo, so they settled on 3.*] and submit it with a few representative photos. Your profile is inserted into one of several big mug books for perusal by the opposite sex. Prospective suitors then look through the books and decide whom they'd like to meet.

One day while examining the books, I subconsciously noticed a photo of a woman on her apartment's balcony overlooking a pool. The reason I say it was subconscious is because 15 minutes later, I thought I saw the exact same woman in a different mug book. I feverishly leafed back through all the books and saw that they were photographs of two different women taken on the same balcony.

Bingo. Randi and Karen had to be roommates who signed up for Profiles together. Of course, they didn't know that I knew, so I did what I had to do. I selected them both as dates.

I knew that Profiles would contact them both on the same day, so I wondered if they'd even accept the invitation to meet. Fortunately, Randi said yes.

It was kind of fun speaking with her on the phone. Several times, she tried to delicately hint that I had also chosen her roommate. I did my best to draw it out by changing the subject whenever I sensed she might mention that I had also selected Karen. When the secret finally came out, it killed all chances of having any kind of relationship with either of them.

Romance Factor: Low. Although some women might have appreciated the chutzpah, most don't like to feel like they're the subjects of an elaborate joke. Furthermore, roommates don't want a man to come between their friendship [*but will if he has a really good career*].

Lesson: It was fun. I'd do it again in a heartbeat.

{ *Definition of Immaturity*:
When playing a prank is more
important than having a relationship.

First Day of Work

I have consulted for an International Investment firm for several years [*If you happen to have an extra $100 million laying around, I can have Churchill, the Executive Vice President give you a call to help you invest it. I can guarantee the money will be at least as safe as putting it in a mattress, (probably even safer!)*] The dress code is a suit and tie.

One Monday morning, I was in the office microwaving pizza at around 8:30 A.M. I happened to be inappropriately dressed in a T-shirt, jeans, and sneakers and had a towel draped over my shoulder. I was planning to change clothes in my office.

On the way, I strolled over to Nicole's desk with a slice of pizza in hand. Since it was her first day of work she was dressed to impress. We had never met. So I welcomed her with, "I can't believe you're wearing that on your first day", then turned and walked away.

Instead of being incredulous or insulted, she just laughed. It was the beginning of a nice friendship.

Romance Factor: Low to moderate. This is really the same as "Welcome to College" since a woman in transition is very approachable.

Lesson: Not only do some women enjoy a good joke, eating pizza in the morning is a good indicator that you aren't otherwise attached.

Lesson #2: Don't microwave pizza for more than 2 minutes. It gets really dry and all the cheese sticks to the turntable.

Patsy

"Move your junk and let me in there!" I said feigning indignance. I always choose a window seat and it seemed like bravado would be a good way to approach the full-figured statuesque bottle-blond that was already in the aisle seat.

My heart sank as she looked up at me crying with big raccoon eyes. Had I hurt her? Did a loved one just die? This was going to be a long flight.

As it turns out, she was crying because her two-year relationship had suddenly ended. A few hours earlier, her man had unceremoniously dropped her at the airport with a one-way ticket to Texas. Since women often enjoy discussing their feelings I asked her if she wanted to talk about it.

We talked for the entire flight. I listened to all the details of her relationship and breakup. And by the end of the flight, she was actually laughing [*I had broccoli in my teeth.*] She handed me her number at the luggage carousel.

Since it was nearing New Year's Eve and she had just been dumped, I was reasonably sure she didn't have a date lined up. And I was certain I didn't, so I asked her out and she accepted.

I took her to a party that a lot of my friends attended. All of them agreed that she was very pretty. However, they also agreed on something else. They all said she was, or at least had at one time been, a man.

All things considered, the evening was pretty enjoyable. In the wee hours of the morning, I had to pull up to the ATM and get some cash. That's when she kissed me for the very first time. [*Note to women: Try not to have your first kiss in front of an ATM. Rewarding a man for withdrawing money to spend on you sets a bad precedent.*]

As this was our only date, I never did find out Patsy's gender. Although if she was a guy, she may just be the most gorgeous man I've ever met.

Romance Factor: Low. It's a bad idea to date anyone a week after their two-year relationship breaks up.

Lesson: Listening is romantic. Everyone wants to be listened to, especially people who are in pain. And it seems like women I date are always in pain from something or someone. Had I not taken the time to listen to her, I would never have gotten the opportunity to be caught kissing her on the Bank's security cameras.

Meeting someone on a plane isn't as good an idea as you think. Most of the people that you'd disqualify after 20 seconds at a party become magically enticing when you are forced captives on a plane. They seem more interested in you because they're stuck with you no matter how weaselly you are. Plus you actually have time to get to know them and discover how similar you both are [*Hey, we both like movies! What are the odds?*]

Of course, once you deboard, and are free of captivity, you often find that you've got nothing in common. And Patsy and I had absolutely nothing in common—except the fact that we were both men.

Do You Want Fries With That?

Next time you're waiting in a fast food drive-thru lane at a fine establishment like Jack In The Box [*which they should call "Jacques du Boîte" to make it sound like they're a smelly French restaurant that most Americans hate, but think is somehow classy*] look in your rear view mirror. There just might be somebody you want to meet in the vehicle behind you. [*Probably Rosie O'Donnell*]

You can wave, but that won't establish any meaningful contact. You can try to get out of your car, but that will not only frighten people, but also ding your precious Silver Beamer that you bought to show how successful you are. Your options are limited and your time is exiguous.

The right move is to pay for the car behind you. Unless this is one of those fast food joints that say, "Busses Welcome", chances are it won't cost more than $10.

Romance Factor: Moderate

Lesson: Unfortunately, this approach borders on being a little too smooth for my tastes. Although you can certainly pique a woman's interest, it's not readily apparent that you're a romantic guy. You could just be a real smooth, greaseball who uses this scam as a matter of course.

That's one big difference between romantic guys and players. A romantic guy would do something like this only once, because romance is about creating a special shared experience unique to the couple. Slick guys have no compunction about using their move dozens of times as standard operating procedure.

Lesson #2: IHOP should call themselves "Maison du Crèpes Internationale".

Caveat: If you meet a woman at the drive-thru, there's a greater than zero chance that she has hidden "fast food hips". But hey, maybe you like that.

2.
Personal Ads
(that don't work)

PERSONAL ADS CAN BE A GREAT WAY TO MEET NEW PEOPLE. However, like any advertising, not all pitches are created equally. You have to be careful and concise because any one of your words may have a hidden connotation. In fact, most people read personal ads looking for a word or phrase that will disqualify you from all the other amazing single people who can't find a date.

I once answered a personal ad from a woman who said she was seeking someone who was spontaneous. So I answered the ad on December 29th and asked her out for New Years Eve. And what do you know? She never returned my call. It seems that she wasn't quite as spontaneous as she liked to think.

The following ads would seemingly work well, but don't.

No Cereal Killers

Cap'n Crunch seeks Just Right Pebbles for some Lucky Charms and Kix. You're Healthwise, enjoy a Variety Pack of life, know your Alpha-Bits and have more than Two Scoops of common sense, but are sometimes Total Nuts. Looking for someone to Teem around with before O's, who's not an Instant Breakfast. Send proof of purchase. No Flakes, Fruit Loops, Pop Tarts, or Trix and no surprises inside the box.

This Personal Ad won Randel "Ad of the Week" and dinner for two at a local restaurant. Unfortunately, no one answered it.

Strong Silent Type

Great Guy

I'm strong, sensitive, and romantic with a lot of integrity, a wonderful career, and a great sense of humor. I'm looking for a woman with similar qualities for a long-term relationship.

3.
Personal Ads
(that work)

ALTHOUGH MOST PERSONAL ADS ARE A LONG SHOT, the ones in this chapter will actually work. Several people may respond to your ad, so you must arbitrarily select your dates based upon little or no information. [*Which is how most people choose a long distance company.*]

Here is an example of a successful ad placed by my friend Susan. In order to increase her odds of success while mitigating her losses in the event of some dating disaster, she placed an ad that briefly described herself and two of her friends. The ad stated that they were looking for three men.

Now they could afford not to subject each respondent to the intense scrutiny of a one-on-one situation. In this way, there was at least a remote chance that 2 of the 6 would have enough in common to start a relationship. Plus they hoped to eliminate a lot of the pressure of two strangers trying to make awkward conversation.

According to Susan, the megadate was fun, but no two of the six ever dated after that. Still, this date has the potential for being very romantic [*To hear this book tell it, so does touring a sewage plant*]. If you do something like this, Susan suggests an activity like mini-golf over something as conversation intensive as dinner. Here are other personal ads that work.

Wealthy Tycoon

Handsome successful professional seeking a woman over 35 that I can spoil. Friends first. Kids OK. Looks not important.

Big Time Loser

Unemployed, greasy-haired, drummer afraid of commitment. Just got out of jail. Looking for a beautiful, intellectual, rich model that will go on the road with me whenever I can get a gig. Must have a car.

Models will actually answer this ad (and then throw up their dinner to look thin for him).

4.
Romantic
Dates (I've had)

DINNER AND A MOVIE. OR MAYBE DINNER AND DANCING. THAT'S IT. That's what a date is supposed to consist of. It's seems to be some kind of rule.

Well it's not a rule. You can be more romantic if you just give your date a little extra thought. In fact, *everything you do* will be that much better if you just devote a little more time and effort to it.

To illustrate: You might really look forward to reading this section if I just gave the introduction a little more thought to make it more compelling.

But that would ruin my whole point, now wouldn't it?

The Laundromat

You know that 16-year-old boy who hasn't quite reached physical maturity? He still looks 12, his voice cracks and he's never shaved. He's awkward. He might as well be 12. [*Bad analogy alert!*]

Sadly this was me, except at 19. I might as well have been 12. Everything that other kids learned about dating in high school completely passed me by.

Oh sure, I had been on a few awkward dinner dates, but I didn't really understand how dating was supposed to work. How did a long, leisurely dinner at a nice restaurant with a total stranger lead to romance? Even more puzzling, how did being quarterback of your high school football team seem to lead to it instantly and without the food?

I met Mary at a frat party and asked her to go to dinner in Chinatown. Of course I could have asked her to go to a movie too [*movies make great dates because you can avoid any real communication for almost two hours, virtually insuring that emotional intimacy will never develop*], but I didn't have enough quarters for the typical theatres in Boston's Chinatown.

We walked there, and on the way we passed a Laundromat. It was then that I was struck with a startling revelation that would change my life: *My underwear was too tight!*

Actually, the revelation was that the dinner charade I had been unsuccessfully copying from TV was not only unoriginal, but was really not all that romantic.

I furtively entered the Laundromat with Mary and bought her a soft drink. [*I actually don't remember which brand of soft drink I bought her, so if you happen to be an opportunistic beverage company executive and would like to pay me to insert your product name into future editions of this book, please contact me with sponsorship details.*] We sat and drank our sodas to completion. I think we were both a little confused about why we were in a Laundromat in the first place. But I knew that dating would never be the same for me again.

We soon departed for Chinatown, ate, and finished our first and last unremarkable date together. Maybe we should have done something more romantic instead, like walk to a fountain, throw coins in and make wishes. But remember, I was like a 12-year-old wearing constrictive Underoos.

Romance Factor: Low for this date because of my general ineptitude in handling the welcome but unexpected turn of events.

A more moderate romance factor can be achieved by bringing a game like Darts or Twister to the facility. Bring some snacks and engage the incredibly bored patrons to participate in your date. Just be careful to make your date the center of your attention. Think up your own Laundromat variation, such as a candlelight dinner.

Lesson: Any pinhead can take a woman to "Dinner and a Movie". It shows absolutely no originality and does nothing to tailor the experience to the woman. Any woman can be plugged into this equation. Romance is about customizing your actions to a particular woman.

For example, when Leatrice's old boyfriend took her to a Wagner Opera, they sat in the back and he made up hilarious dialogue for the duration of the presentation. [*Only do this if you're hilarious—which you're not if you like opera*].

If you want to differentiate yourself from others (you do) take a chance and try something out of the ordinary. Even if she ends up thinking you're a dork (you are) at least you'll both come away with a story to tell your friends.

Apple Picking

There is something about picking apples on a cool, crisp autumn day in New England that oozes romance. West Coast natives consider picking apples to be manual labor, and not in the least bit romantic.

But I beg to differ. It is one of the most romantic dates you can have.

The day is spent walking up and down the rows of the orchard until you find a secluded spot where you can relax under a tree, gaze up at billowy cumulus clouds, hold hands, and eat the best tasting, freshest apples available. It positively stirs the soul. Bringing some good cheese, crusty bread, and a wine skin won't hurt either, unless you hate wine, like I do.

Although Karen and I were nearing the end of our relationship, the day we went apple picking was one of the finest, most enjoyable, romantic dates I've ever had. In fact, we specifically waited until the date was over before our inevitable break-up.

Romance Factor: High. When you go apple picking, tell her you'll bake an apple pie for her. If she knows you're a lousy cook, she might offer to do this for you. She may even offer to cook you an entire meal to go along with it. Score!

Lesson: You cannot possibly eat a bushel of apples, even if you give a metric ton of them away.

Barry Manilow

Back in my "Summer of non-commitment" [*One chapter in my "Life of Non-Commitment", I guess*], I spent a fair amount of time with a good-hearted woman with a great sense of humor named Kathy. Part of the reason we got along so well was because we shared many dysfunctions, one being the inexplicable love of Barry Manilow music.

When Barry came to town on his Showstopper tour, we got tickets to the show far in advance. Since neither of us ever had seen him, we were excited by the concert. Furthermore, this was an opportunity to enjoy his music without feeling like total wieners.

But by the time the concert rolled around, Kathy was starting to hate me because I was sending her mixed messages. That morning, Chiz approached me, said he had great tickets to a (Bird era) Celtics game, and invited me to go along.

Talk about a dilemma! Well it's not hard to guess that any wussy who writes a romance book would end up at the Manilow concert because that's what you do when you have plans with someone.

Romance Factor: High. Despite any acrimony Kathy and I might have been experiencing, going to the concert was the right thing to do. Plus, I finally got to hear "I Write the Songs". [*Which ironically wasn't written by Barry Manilow, but by Bruce Johnston.*]

Lesson: Mixed messages and non-commitment are poison for any relationship, be it romantic, platonic, or even business.

This harkens back to the Cardinal Rule of Romance. When you make a date, keep it. If nothing else, it shows you are a man of honor [*who has awful taste in music*].

The Airport Game

[Note: this idea originated from a movie some time around 1980.]

This date requires you to do a little bit of research either by calling airlines or surfing the Internet. The fact that there's some preparation will end up disqualifying most guys.

Your first task is to find about 4 flights on different airlines that arrive 20 minutes after one another. Create an itinerary and tell your date to be at the specified security checkpoint at the times specified in the itinerary. At no time tell her what you're up to. Just e-mail her the itinerary.

Go to the airport. When the passengers start arriving, you blend into the stream of those deplaning and scream in excitement when you see her. That's when the passionate kissing begins. Bring balloons or confetti or clown shoes to make the event even more special. Then, when you've sickened all the weary travelers on the flight, meet up at the next flight and repeat. Hopefully, you've planned ahead and hired a limo to bring you back to town.

I tried this date with Debbie many years ago and although it was fun, it didn't work as well as I might have liked. She was fairly reluctant because I had tipped her off as to what we were doing. Also, I was a little shy about making a scene, which kind of defeats the whole point of this date.

In retrospect, it would have been better to just give her the itinerary and tell her to show up at a particular time with no other information.

Romance Factor: High, if executed properly

Lesson: Commit to the idea. Your enthusiasm will pull you through. It's not the kissing that's romantic. Presumably, you can find a place and time to kiss, unfettered by other constraints.

The important part is being in public. The airport is one of the few places you can cause a scene and lasciviously demonstrate that you're not afraid to show her that you care.

This might make a nice date for the day before Thanksgiving when film crews at airports abound.

Airplane Dinner Party

I'm a lousy cook. Unfortunately, that prevents me from fixing my date a delicious romantic dinner in front of the fireplace. [*So does not having a fireplace or a date.*]

I do know how to microwave though. If only there were some way to serve my date a microwaveable dinner in a romantic fashion. That's when I decided upon the airline dinner theme.

The key here is to notice that many frozen dinners are packaged in small white oval/rectangular trays, remarkably similar to those served on airlines. Perfect. I invited my date, Sharon and a bunch of my friends over.

In preparation, I obtained 6 *oz.* plastic cups, ice, square cocktail napkins, and of course, the microwaveable dinners. To add authenticity, I brought barf bags from my collection. [*Check out the Air Sickness Bag Museum: http://www.airsicknessbags.com*]

There were six of us in all. My friend Slammer, who was an Air Force ROTC, wore his uniform and brought small bags of peanuts for everyone.

It all made for an enjoyable and unforgettable dinner party. Luckily, no one had occasion to use the air sickness bags. And the best part about it: *absolutely no cooking!*

Romance Factor: High.

Lesson: The best way to execute this date is to produce more and more airplane related paraphernalia as the dinner progresses. Start by seating people in rows. Distribute in-flight magazines and Safety Cards. [*Like you have some handy.*] Then Peanuts. Drinks. Dinner. Coffee. You know the drill.

If you have a serving cart, all the better. Make sure to bring a big plastic trash bag into the dining area to clear away cups and napkins. Try clearing the table with a big plastic trash bag at a traditional dinner party!

If you're really smooth, excuse yourself toward the end of the meal. From whatever room you go to, you can call out to her in a PA voice, "The captain would like to see you in the cockpit".

The TRAAM

I met Helen at an America On-Line party of all places. It was February 1996 and few people, much less women, were online and they certainly weren't going to geeky AOL parties. [*I was, of course.*] After assaulting her with suave e-moves, I asked for, and got, her e-mail address. We met a few times for lunch. Then we decided to go on our first real date.

I picked her up and we started driving. I ignored her questions about our destination. My only concern about this secrecy was that she might think I was an ax murderer since, after all, we did meet at an AOL party.

"It looks like we're going to the airport", she said, anticipation brewing. Then, a few minutes later, "We are going to the airport".

I parked in the Delta terminal lot and unloaded a boom box, TV table, and grocery sack. We went over to the airport tram [*Which American Airlines called the* TRAAM, *but now calls the* TRAAIN *because they felt the need to burn a lot of money on a pointless name change over making flights run on time*] and got into a car full of passengers.

"We're here!" She was confused. She probably thought I was a generous guy who might buy her love with an impromptu trip to some exotic destination like Hawaii. But I'm not, so I opened the TV table and started pulling Brie, crackers and bubbly [*Champagne, not Mr. Bubble, although I maintain that Mr. Bubble could be a more romantic product on an airport tram, if used properly.*] out of the bag.

As travelers boarded, we'd tell them that this was our first date (it was). We were treated to one of two responses. Either the passengers were very friendly and incredulous or they'd look upon us in disdain and distance themselves as far away from us as possible. No one reacted with indifference [*except Helen*].

After circling the airport about five times [*kind of like flying into* LAX], we had finished dinner and some space had opened up in the car. This was a great opportunity to pop in the Johnny Mathis tape I had purchased specifically for the occasion. And we started to dance.

As fate would have it, a booming authoritative voice shook the driverless TRAAM. From somewhere in the airport, a power hungry TRAAM Cop's voice piped over the loud speaker "Get out [*Obviously modeling his authoritarian mien after Arnold Schwartznegger*] of the car now". The TRAAM stopped at the next stop and would not continue until we deboarded. We had been bounced off an airport tram.

Helen was vocal and confrontational, standing up to the faceless voice with barbs of her own. I erroneously assumed this meant she was having a good time. Rather it was more indicative of her intolerance for authority. I never saw her again, although I maintain to this day that she enjoyed the date.

Romance Factor: High. Sharing risks makes you co-conspirators.

Lesson: Every woman I've ever met from Buffalo—Mary, Lusty Lori, Michelle, Jeanette, and Helen—is pretty. Not all of them have annoying voices though.

Lesson #2: Johnny Mathis is great! My parents' generation really had good taste in romantic music. [*But they sure didn't understand Rock 'n' Roll the way we do. Hoo boy, we sure are rebels!*]

Clothes Shopping

If I've learned one thing about romance, it's that women go crazy for a sharp-dressed man. [*All I really need to know about romance, I learned from ZZ Top.*] It doesn't really seem to matter if he's average looking, as long he's well dressed. While the average guy can get some idea of what's in style by reading magazines like GQ or the Target circular, you quickly find that the word "stylish" varies from woman to woman. [*Watch the Academy Awards some time.*]

Many women like to think of men as their own personal Ken Dolls and dress them up. Sad to say, my wardrobe is almost entirely composed of clothing given to me by women who felt my wardrobe needed to be "upgraded". In fact, I am often criticized for wearing something that was given to me by another woman, who in turn bought it for me because she didn't like the item the woman before her gave me.

Recognizing the critical importance of clothing, and the fact that many women enjoy shopping, I decided to take the bull by the horns. Hoping to ingratiate myself to Trisha [*the bull*], I asked her to go shopping with me.

We set a date. I chose an arbitrary purchasing limit of $200 [*thinking that this was enough to remake my entire wardrobe*] and went off to buy clothes that she selected.

We spent an enjoyable day together and bought a number of items that I currently refer to as "pseudo-Trishwear". "Trishwear" would indicate she had she purchased the items for me.

Strangely enough, she actually had a romantic surprise of her own for me. She brought along "The Book of Questions"; a book containing tough hypothetical questions that challenge your integrity. I know that's not as fun to most people as drinking tequila shots out of each other's shoes or watching a movie about the mob that we all can relate to. [*I love mob movies because they're so relevant to my life—you know, drugs, extortion, murder.*] But I thought that whipping out the book was pretty romantic and a good way to get to know each other.

However, this was to be our last date, despite the fact that her legacy lives on through my clothing.

Romance Factor: Moderate.

Lesson: The romantic thing about having her choose your clothes is that it shows her that you value her opinions and tastes. Furthermore, it demonstrates that you care about your appearance. And finally, you get to spend half the day with your pants down! [*Which you probably already do anyway if your last name is Clinton.*]

Tree Climbing

Liz was raised in Baltimore and never learned to climb trees while growing up. One day, I asked her on a date to go out for a walk [*Translation: I'm really cheap*]. I had her wear sneakers and long pants because, well maybe I'm a controlling megalomaniac.

The plan was actually quite simple. Go out and climb trees. When I sprung the plan on her, she was game and loved the date.

Now it may take a bit of convincing before your acrophobic date climbs her first tree. If that's the case, just find a tree and climb it without her.

She'll want to get in that tree with you. It's monkey see, monkey do. Some evolutionary trait developed long ago in the African forest canopy compels humans to climb trees [*and watch pro wrestling*].

Maybe you can convince her to climb the tree by extending your hand. This is a purely natural and benevolent way for you to initiate physical contact with her. If she exhibits any trepidation about getting in the tree, you might have to find yourself a hairier woman with a big forehead and prehensile tail.

Romance Factor: Moderate. High if she happens to be wearing a dress and climbs anyway. Low if you happen to be wearing a dress.

Lesson: A woman that likes challenges, self-improvement and independence will love this date.

Tree Climbing with a Surprise

For my next date with Liz, I told her in advance that we would be climbing trees. She embraced this idea as an opportunity to have fun and continue to develop her tree climbing acumen.

I mentioned that there was a particular tree I wanted her to climb. So we drove to a local park and walked over to that tree.

My criteria for choosing this tree was that it had to be:

— *Climbable by a novice*

— *Publicly visible to pedestrians*

— *Easily accessible by motor vehicle*

The tree was located at the end of a parking lot and its branches spread out over a well-used bike trail. Perfect.

Although the tree was a little difficult to climb, we both managed to handle it OK. Facing a tricky descent, she asked, "How are we going to get down?" [*No, Liz isn't black.*] I told her not to worry about it now, and that she should just make herself comfortable.

The timing just happened to be impeccable. Within 5 minutes, a pizza delivery guy showed up. For the rest of the date, we sat up in the tree eating pizza as we elicited curious gazes and inquisitive conversation from runners, rollerbladers, and cyclists below.

Romance Factor: High

Recommendation: Set this up beforehand. Pizza delivery shops don't have maps of where all the good climbing trees are. Plus they're reticent to deliver to a park, since it makes them susceptible to robbery.

Recommendation 2: For more tree romance, get a hammock and spend the night sleeping in a tree with her.

Lesson: Pizza Hut has lousy pizza, but at least they'll deliver to a tree.

Boo!

The fact is that Haunted Houses are romantic, dark, hand-holding opportunities that only operate for a short period of the year. Unfortunately however, not all are created equally so you have to be both judicious and lucky to choose the right one. You see, while Margaret and I visited one that was enjoyable, it was not scary enough to elicit sufficient fear to draw her under my protective wing.

So I committed the cardinal sin of repeating a date with two different women on consecutive nights. It was probably unconscionable, but I did it nonetheless.

The following evening, I took Cathy to a different Haunted House. The level of terror here was just right. It was high enough to initiate physical contact, but low enough so that we weren't overwhelmed with fear or nightmares.

Incidentally, Cathy almost called and canceled the date the night we went out. She sensed some personality quirks in me that made her skeptical of us having a successful relationship. She showed up anyway and after the date, decided that I was worth a shot. Eight months later, of course, she came full circle to hate me again, although I'm not exactly sure why. [*Of course I don't know why. I'm a guy!*]

Romance Factor: Moderate. It's a common date, thereby lowering its romantic appeal.

Lesson: Even though romance requires individual attention, maybe it's worth another shot. You know, 3 strikes and you're out.

We Deliver For You

One of the most, if not the most romantic dates I ever had was at the local Post Office. The lobby is open 24 hours and contains a huge circular table upon which to conduct postal business. I pre-made a dinner for Liz and loaded the food, a few barstools, and a boom box in the trunk. Then I went over to pick her up.

"Hey, before I tell you where we're going, I need to go to the Post Office and mail this letter." She never suspected anything until after I mailed the letter. That's when I started pulling bar stools out of the trunk and carrying them up to the table inside. Finally, I just said, "We're here".

We went in and ate dinner. This being a post office, there was a huge floor plan to accommodate the long lines they usually have. We asked postal customers who randomly walked in to do afterhours postal business to serenade us and we'd dance. Usually, we tried to get them to sing, "We're your postal service, we deliver for you". But one romantic woman actually knew all the lyrics to "I Could Have Danced All Night" [*She was obviously a mutant of some sort*], and sang it to us while we danced.

We weighed our food on the metering machine to determine how much it would cost to send it to our distant friends so they could share the experience with us. I didn't bring any alcohol or candles, figuring it would be against some federal regulation to do so.

So I would say if you're looking for a romantic date, find a post office and go for it.

Romance Factor: High. An advanced and very expensive version of this date would be the Post Office "Automat". This would require you to buy several post office boxes [*At the low, low price of $32 per box for six months*] and load food in each one before the date. Then hand your date a bunch of keys and let her find dinner.

Just for kicks, leave a little something in one of the PO boxes for the postal workers to find. A glass of milk or a couple of sardines works great.

Lesson: If you've read this far into the book, it's time to get up. Somebody else probably wants to use the bathroom.

We'll Kiss For Food

Women often have a soft spot for doing benevolent deeds. If a man participates in such altruistic pursuits, women will consider him a caring individual worthy of their interest.

Many women also love to receive attention, and Denise is no exception. And when she gets that attention, it's important to her to be dressed appropriately. So on Valentine's Day, I told her to prepare to be outside for two hours, to wear comfortable shoes, and to wear something that she wouldn't mind having lots of people see her in.

We pulled into Denny's parking lot. "Are we going to Denny's?" "No, but we can later if you like." Those were not the words she wanted to hear on Valentine's Day, as I unpacked the goody sack, a bar stool, and 2 pieces of cardboard.

We walked over to the busy median strip and set up. I opened a bottle of champagne and poured us each a glass. Then I gave her a large cardboard sign that said: *Happy Valentines!*

My sign said: *We'll Kiss For Food. (Donations go to Charity)*

When cars would pull up to the stoplight and give us a dollar, I'd throw down my sign, run to Denise, dip her and kiss her passionately. Although she was uneasy about the whole thing [*she was kissing me, after all*] she was being a pretty good sport about it.

Then, about 30 minutes into the date, an SUV pulled onto the median strip. The Fox 4 News crew showed up! Good old Fox. They recognize a scoop. [*I tipped them off the day before. The Dallas Morning News however, wanted nothing to do with the story.*] They filmed us for a while and put us on the News that evening. In fact, we were the tease they used to get people to stay tuned.

Not only were we featured on TV, we raised about $25 for "The Family Place", a local battered woman's shelter.

After the date was over, Denise confided that what she was really hoping for was what society tells her she should want: flowers and dinner. Now that really would have showed my love for her. Flowers and dinner may have taken almost a full five minutes to plan!

Romance Factor: High

Lesson: Media exposure can cure almost any ill. People love to be on TV. Just watch a crowd shot at any sporting event to verify this assertion.

Lesson #2: Being homeless and holding a sign on the street corner has to be really awful.

5.
Romantic
Dates (I want to have)

THERE SEEMS TO BE AN INEXHAUSTIBLE REALM of romantic dates to be had. Here are some that I've always wanted to do. It's a good idea to visualize the entire date first. Then daydream about it. Then daydream some more. [*OSHA Warning: Don't operate heavy machinery when you do this*]

Only then will you have the conviction to pull it off successfully and romantically, since there may be several unexpected turns of events. Since these dates haven't actually happened, you can create your own endings and draw your own conclusions.

Discovery Zone

Kids love Discovery Zone because of all the tunnels, slides, ladders, and pits filled with plastic balls and foam. However, kids aren't the only ones who like it. Many adults enjoy cargo nets, too. [*How else do you explain the popularity of American Gladiators?*]

The confounding thing is that Discovery Zone only allows adults into the facility accompanied by a child. Which means if you want to take a date there, you're out of luck—unless you already have children together—in which case you probably hate each other and will do just about anything to avoid going on dates together.

My friend Tex has been trying to sell me on how romantic it would be to take a date to Discovery Zone. Unselfishly, he is happy to provide me with one or more of his children in order to gain admittance.

I have not as yet taken him up on this date, but plan to in the future. I can't wait to slide into the vat o' plastic balls, discover my date hiding in there, and kiss her.

And just as we experience our first passionate embrace, a big explosion occurs! [*Well, not really, but upon reflection, this date wasn't sounding very compelling. Whenever a Hollywood movie needs help, they put in some kind of explosion, usually a helicopter.*]

Romance Factor: Low to Moderate. If your date has been experiencing powerful maternal urges, or already has kids, it's romantic to know that you love kids too. However be forewarned little Mboto will probably get in the way of that juicy kiss.

Lesson: Never accept romance advice from a 5' 7" Jewish attorney named Tex. However, you would be a moron not to accept legal advice from him.

Pet Birthday

Back around 1994, when Brian, Dave, and I thought we'd be good at writing sitcom scripts, [*The networks thought otherwise, of course*] we wrote a couple episodes of Seinfeld. One of the scripts had a story line about a birthday party for a dog and the wacky hilarity that ensues when you crash one.

I believe throwing a birthday for a woman's pet would make a compelling and romantic date. It would work best with a dog, but could work with any pet.

This date requires a little bit of planning. [*Don't plan too far in advance for a goldfish.*] Invite all of her friends who have pets and get a cake that says, "Happy 7th [*or 14th or 21st or whatever*] Birthday". Then, on her pet's actual birthday, gather everyone together, and when she and her pet enter, yell "Surprise!" I guarantee the pet will be surprised. Although this is a birthday party for her pet, it's really a surprise party for her.

Romance Factor: High. It may not be the most intimate date you ever have, but it will be a lot of fun.

Lesson: This date demonstrates that you not only care about her, but care about her pet, who is presumably very near and dear to her. After all, her relationship with her pet has probably lasted longer than any relationship she's ever had with a man [*because her pet can't leave the relationship*].

Advanced Laundromat

This is a great date if you happen to have a Tuxedo that needs dry cleaning. You should also be prepared for your date to be extremely disappointed for a good portion of the evening. [*If you're not prepared for this, don't even think about getting married.*]

You will first need to buy some Dryel. For those who missed their aggressive ad campaign, Dryel is a product that allows you to dry clean clothing yourself in regular commercial clothes dryers.

Tell your date to get dressed up in really nice clothing, as if you're going to a fancy restaurant. Show up in shorts or jeans and a T-shirt, but under no circumstances let her change clothes after she sees you. She has to trust you after all.

Go to a really seedy Laundromat where she'll feel completely out of place [*you hope*]. Preferably, the Laundromat has a public bathroom. You can make a pitiful effort to quell her discomfort by producing a carnation or a greeting card or something lame like that.

Pull out your Dryel bag with the Tux inside and surreptitiously throw it in the dryer, not letting her see what's inside. As far as she knows, you asked her to get all dressed up just to go to the Laundromat and do your laundry. Now just sit back and chat. This is when you have to be strong and not let her extreme disappointment get to you.

Wait for all the cycles to finish. [*Dryer cycles, not her…oh never mind.*] Then excuse yourself to the bathroom and emerge in the freshly cleaned Tuxedo. [*Hint: Don't bring one of those Tuxedo T-Shirts*]. Now it's time to sweep her off her feet.

Rescue her from the Laundromat. Head directly to the Symphony, Ballet, Opera or other intolerable artsy venue that costs a fortune yet isn't even compelling enough to be carried by any of the 863 cable channels you get.

Although she will probably love this date, whatever you do, make sure a huge explosion occurs!

Romance Factor: High.

Lesson: Trust is romantic and in this date you demonstrably show her that she can trust you and your judgement in the face of what appears to be grave disappointment.

Santa Trifecta

Kelley and I just got back from our 3rd annual search for gaudy, life-sized, animatronic Santas that people put up around the end of the year. For the third year in a row, we successfully landed the Santa Trifecta, although this year it took over an hour to find three of them.

Now I'm the last person that would ever get excited about Christmas hype, but that doesn't mean I don't like to look at decorations. So one night, Kelley and I came up with the idea of a scavenger hunt.

A scavenger hunt would make a fine date. Just draw up a list of decorations to find, give a few other couples the list, and after an hour or two, see who comes up with the most items on the list. Bring an instant camera to document your findings.

A typical list might include:
— *A tree lit only in blue lights*
— *10 Yard Snowmen*
— *5 angels composed only of lights*
— *A tree on someone's roof*
— *A house with a candle in each window*
— *A "Ho Ho Ho" Quinella*
— *And, of course, the Santa Trifecta*

Romance Factor: Low to Moderate

Lesson: A scavenger hunt gives you a common purpose and gets you working together as a team. Plus, you will learn valuable lessons about your compatibility when you see how your date handles competition.

WWW

Back when I was in Boy Scouts, I was part of a "secret" order of individuals known as "The Order of the Arrow". [*Motto: Weemachendink, Wingolaushik, Witahemawei—really! Sorry if I spoiled the big secret.*] Although it's kind of an honor to be inducted, some cynics say the organization was formed to give scout camps a free slave labor pool.

In order to make new inductees feel honored rather than exploited, my old Boy Scout camp (Stratton Mountain Scout Reservation in Vermont) used to hold a very moving induction ceremony. At nightfall, three canoes would appear on the pond in the distance with torches blazing on their bows as they paddled silently towards shore. The paddlers, dressed in Native American ceremonial garb, would land, select new members of the order from the crowd, and whisk them away to the secret society's day-long induction.

This would make an incredible date. I had the entire thing planned out when I lived on Lake Archer with Craig. I was going to invite Gayle down for a date one moonless night, giving no clue as to what our plans might be.

When she got to the lake, I would explain that I would speak very little, if at all, for the rest of the evening. I would be wearing only the following: some kind of loincloth [*optional for a stud like you*], a pair of sandals, and ankle bracelets with bells on them, just to give the date that Cro-Magnon feel you're always reading about.

Then I'd then lead her through the woods, barking out one-word instructions such as "follow". When I eventually led her to shore across the lake, I'd give her a beverage and say "patience". Then I'd hand her a second beverage and say "much patience".

I'd run away back down the trail so that my bells would be the only things breaking the silence. I would go back to the house and set up a tablecloth, candles and dinner on the dock.

Then I'd get in the canoe and paddle across the lake. As I approached, I'd light my torch (a tree branch with an old shirt dipped in kerosene or whatever). Then I'd approach the shore and pick her up.

I'd paddle her back to the dock, light the candles, and say, "eat". I would maintain silence throughout the entire experience, adding to the date's mystique.

Naturally, she dumped me before any of this ever happened.

Romance Factor: High, but scary. Leaving a woman alone unattended in unfamiliar territory heightens her awareness and sensations.

Lesson: I think I have some sort of personality disorder.

Restaurant in the Woods

I was out walking in the woods one day and came upon a clearing near the bank of a river. Someone had placed two chairs upon the bank. I found this oasis to be a wonderful secluded place to relax.

That's the genesis for the restaurant in the woods. This date requires a fair amount of preparation. You'll need to first find a pleasant isolated place in the woods. Then bring a couple of chairs, a table, dishes, candles and food there. Print up 2 menus, and get two friends to carry it all into the woods. Hire students if you have no friends. [*But don't hire an escort if you don't have a date*]

Tell your date that you're taking her for an evening walk in the woods. Bring a flashlight. Try to synchronize your arrival with your friends so that they light the candles just before you arrive. When you get there, have one of your friends seat you and the other give you menus. They will do waiter stuff. You know, bring you food, clear off dishes, spill coffee on you etc.

Romance Factor: High.

Lesson: This date will work partially because of the amount of preparation it takes, demonstrating that she's important enough for you to spend time on and rope your friends into. It will also work because it's shared among more than just the two of you. The third factor working for you is the isolation and exhilarating experience of eating in the woods.

E-Food

No, not food you click on. E-Food is how my old running partner Amy and I referred to Ethiopian Food. [*We abbreviated many common phrases. For instance, Banana Pudding became "Ban Pud". We didn't shorten Butterscotch Pudding though.*]

As you probably know, Ethiopian restaurants don't provide utensils when they serve you dinner. You tear off some Injera (sponge-like bread) in your hand and pinch it around the E-Food to scoop it up.

Some people find eating at an Ethiopian restaurant awkward. Consider how much more awkward it would be if you were handcuffed to your date.

The reason I have yet to execute this plan is because it works best only when your date favors a different hand than you. So if you're right handed and she's a lefty, you're all set for an evening of fun and compromise, sitting side by side, eating with your hands, and getting lentils in your nose.

Romance Factor: Moderate. The more crowded the restaurant, the more glaring the looks you will elicit. Even better, pull that orange prisoner's jump suit out of your closet and wear it.

Lesson: Unless your car has bench seats, wait until after you're out of the car to affix the manacles.

Flip a Coin Hike

"What do you want to do tonight?"

"I don't know, what do you want to do?"

Chances are your night will include dinner somewhere. So why not let your plans be determined by a coin flip or a roll of the dice? [*Me and my gambling addiction.*]

This date is an amalgamation of my friend Jeff's "party for your car" and the "flip a coin hike" from the 1973 Boy Scout Handbook.

If you take the subway or light rail, flip a coin before you board to determine your direction of travel. Once on the train, roll the dice. That's how many stops you'll go. [*Don't bring your nerdy Dungeons and Dragons icosahedron dice or you'll never get off the train.*]

Then when you deboard, you can flip or roll to determine which direction and how far you go. At every intersection, flip or roll again. You can make up your own rules of travel. For instance, maybe you flip two coins. Two heads is a right, two tails is a left, and otherwise it's straight.

If you drive, use the coin for turns and the dice for the number of blocks to go. There are limitless combinations. Just find one that works for you.

Romance Factor: Low to Moderate, depending upon where fate lands you. Here, the uncertainty of the destination is the fun.

I have actually used this algorithm [*I love the fact that I can justify using the word "algorithm" in a book about romance*] when The Bulgemobile (my first car) flipped 100,000 miles. Six of my friends and I started at home and flipped coins, turning when the coins told us to.

We kept doing this until the car turned over 100,000 miles, at which time we parked The Bulgemobile and had some champagne. [*Ironically, the odometer turned over in the parking lot of an alcohol detox unit.*]

Lesson: Surprise is the major romantic selling point here. Don't invite a xenophobic control freak on this date. If you randomly end up at a terrible restaurant in an unsavory neighborhood [i.*e. any suburb, like Plano, TX for instance*] you will scare control freaks who easily fall out of their comfort zones and blame you for their anxiety.

Anyone Can Be on TV

When I moved to Dallas in 1992, a stand-up comedian named Gary invited me to be on and write for his live Cable Access TV Show called Open Season. The only reason the community at large can broadcast at all is because of concessions cable companies made with the public in order to get their foot in the door back in the 70's. If you take a few 2-hour classes and pay the cable access station $50, you too can produce your own TV show.

On one show, Gary decided to lampoon the other less than compelling programming found on community access cable. The sketch featured excerpts from fake shows like "Ironing With Bill", "Stuff in My Apartment", and "Hey, We're Sitting Around".

So why not have a show of your own with your date as the star? The way it works is to line up a camera operator, board op and maybe gaffer (people need to perform these functions in order to get certified, so they're readily available). Take your date down to the studio and put her on set. This is when she learns that the show is called "Community Access Kissing". Then you just kiss for a half an hour.

As this is Cable Access, you can punctuate the action with a few Public Service Announcements about say, the spread of infectious diseases.

Romance Factor: High, if she's an exhibitionist.

Lesson: Don't be afraid to kiss on TV because nobody ever watches Cable Access. Not even the people that appear on it.

Reverse Halloween

If the fact that you are too old to go trick or treating in any way distresses you, take heart. The "trick" part is often overlooked. As an adult, you can dress up to go trick or treating, simplify your life, make others happy, make it all into a romantic date and even get some free candy to boot.

You'll need to do some preparation, however. The first thing you'll need to do is make a costume. This isn't terribly onerous, but you really can't skip this step.

Next, check around your house for stuff you don't need. Clean out the garage, look through old magazines, check in drawers, and gather the junk you don't want. Skip heavy stuff like furniture and bowling balls. [*okay, you can bring 3 – 5 of your bowling balls if you really want*] Make sure you and your date can carry all the stuff at the same time.

When Halloween rolls around, get in costume, bring all your expendables, and go trick or treating. When your surprised neighbors open the door and see you, offer them any one of your items in exchange for candy. Everyone will love it because people love free stuff. [*Your date loves free candy, multi-millionaires love free stadiums etc.*]

Romance Factor: High. Unfortunately, the one thing this date lacks is the element of surprise, although the anticipation more than compensates.

Lesson: The ability to incite feelings of nostalgia into a date is rare and romantic. Part of being romantic is making her feel like a child again. Some people try to regain this feeling by going to the circus, [*or buying a sports car if you're a middle aged male*] but unlike the circus, Reverse Halloween has costumes, is participatory, and is completely clown-free.

Sousa Picnic

Most high schools and grade schools have a marching band. And you are going to use that marching band as your entertainment. If you don't know a band instructor, it's a good idea to make one's acquaintance. I'm not sure how best to do this, but I have a theory that music teachers congregate at creepy Mensa meetings and Star Trek Conventions.

Find out when the marching band has practice. About 15 minutes before the time rolls around, spread a blanket on the field and start your picnic. Within moments, the marching band should appear. They will simultaneously serenade you with loud marching music and make formations around your picnic. If you're on good terms with the bandleader, he or she would probably be happy to work around your schedule.

While this may seem romantic, it isn't going to be good enough. You should also make friends with the chemistry teacher, because then, a big explosion can occur.

Romance Factor: Moderate. It's probably not as romantic as the hackneyed violin serenade, but it's more fun.

Lesson: Man, there sure are a lot of fat kids in the marching band!

6. Romance Every Day

ROMANCE IS SIMPLY THIS. Remembering her, and more important, showing her that you remember her. Let her know she's always in your thoughts.

This doesn't mean remembering that she hasn't done your laundry. This means being appreciative of her on a regular, but sporadic basis. [*For physicists that don't understand what I mean by this, pretend that your actions are photons. They occur with statistical regularity, but happen unpredictably at any given time. Hey, romance is stochastic!*]

Here's a list of things you can do to be romantic. While some of the actions on this list can be done only once or twice, many of them can be done over and over in different forms.

Remember your monthly anniversary with a phone call, e-mail, flower on her door, card in her purse, or dedication on her favorite radio station

Always send thank you cards when she gets you a gift

Instead of calling her up when you're courting her, have your friends call her up to impress her with interesting factoids about you

Send her letters from in town,
just to say hello—even if you live together

Send her flowers with a mushy note

Send her flowers with an edgy note, such as "I love you so much, I had these killed on your behalf." If you always send mushy love notes, she'll consider you a wimp. [*If you bought this book, you are.*] Showing emotion is fine, but not always. She still wants to occasionally think of you as the insensitive, unfeeling man you are. Every woman wants a man that's a little bit bad.

Bring her a flower when you see her

Bring her flour when you see her

Bring her flower seeds when you see her. Tell her that you hope you're together when they produce flowers, like Dan did. [*Then, after you've gained her trust, steal all her stuff, like Dan also did.*]

Tell her that you love her
Tell her that you love her
Tell her that you love her
Tell her that you love her cooking. But don't lie about loving her cooking if you don't. My friend Seth's father has eaten bananas for 25 years, even though he doesn't like them, but said he did a long time ago. So Seth's mother continues to buy them and he continues to choke them down quietly...

Send her E-cards

Send her a FedEx to say you love her. This should indicate how urgent your love for her is. [*Don't use* UPS *because they'll never get it to her. Then they'll send it back to you after 3 lame delivery attempts*]

Clear the table, do the dishes and wash the laundry. Don't bother folding it because she'll end up re-doing it anyway.

Take dance lessons with her. *you* ask HER.

Give her the big half of your dessert. She'll melt over your generosity and will probably give you back the larger half anyway. No woman wants to appear to be a fat pig. [*She is, in her mind.*]

Eat outside with her when possible

Give her the remote for an entire evening.
Don't even think about touching it [*or the remote*].

Leave the seat down [*duh!*]. If this is where you
draw the line in the sand, you are petty and small.

Leave the seat up on rare occasion. This will prevent her from taking you for granted by reminding her how lucky she is to be with you. [*Hey, I'm not above manipulation.*]

Answer the door dressed as a super-hero. I first met Sween-Monster when I answered the doorbell dressed in a cape and blue tights.

Exercise with her. This not only shows you support her, but you will both look better to boot. Plus you'll implicitly let her know that you care about how you appear to her.

Sing to her, even if you're a lousy singer

Don't always sing romantic songs. You'll start sounding like a wimp. Greg liked to sing the Grossman's Lumber song. You know the one: *There's a little Grossman's in everyone. There's a little Grossman's in you.* [*This probably works really well for a guy I know named Randy Grossman.*]

Fill the coffee maker every night before going to sleep.
Put in hazelnut coffee once in a while.

Make the bed, especially if you're her guest. Leave a mint on the pillow.

Sneak out in the middle of the night to get her a gift

Wash her hair in the sink

Put love notes on her mirror

Rub her feet
[*Wash your hands afterwards*]

Have your portrait made together

Tell her that she's beautiful, but only if she is.

Buy her favorite ice cream and sneak it into her freezer

Blindfold her once in a while when you take her out to dinner. Surprise her with a new restaurant.

Make her something symbolic, like a
Dream Catcher, which Kelly made for Dave.

Brush your teeth once in a while when you wake up to go to the bathroom in the middle of the night.

Buy a new article of clothing for yourself, even if you don't need or want it. Many women partially define themselves by how you look. You care about her looks. She cares about how you dress.

Always drop her off and pick her up at the airport.
Walk off the plane with flowers when she picks you up at the airport

Send her a postcard when out of town

Send her a note telling you how much you miss her
and mail it the day you leave town

Go
for
walks
in the rain

Take her out to feed the ducks

Stop whatever you're doing to hold her and look at the moon

Walk her to her car

Open doors for her, literally and romantically

When you drop her off at her car, make
sure her engine starts before pulling away

When you drop her off at home, make sure she's inside before you leave

When you're out walking together in the spring, sniff the tree blossoms

If you leave hair in the sink, remove it. [*Gather it all up, go in to work before anyone else shows up, and spread the hair around the sink in the ladies room.*]

Don't let a day go by without some
form of communication with her.

Say *Goodnight* and *Good Morning* even if you have to call her to do so

Make sure the last voice she hears before going to sleep is yours rather than some pathetic TV loser like Joey from Friends

7. Romance After Marriage

8.
Romantic Gifts

GIFTS ARE A GREAT WAY OF DEMONSTRATING not only that you care for her, but that you listen to her and more importantly, understand her. Most guys will get women safe gifts if they get them gifts at all.

You can probably reel off half a dozen safe gifts: Jewelry, Flowers, Wine, and Perfume. [*Why not just blurt out, "God, you stink!"?*] And Jewelry. And more Jewelry makes 6. I'm not saying don't give these as gifts. But why not get her something tailored to her? It's nice to be a little lavish with her, but if you don't have money, consider doing an errand or service for her.

Some gifts you might get her:

Make a donation to a charity in her name

Take her car and give her a full tank of gas

Give her a massage. Expect nothing in return.

Get her a massage [*I never do this. Even though women love it, I don't believe in paying some slimeball, who calls his lewd groping "massage", to fondle someone I care about.*]

If you're musically inclined, compose and play an original score for her, like Karen did for me 15 years ago. [*Helpful tip: Don't use a kazoo.*] It's still one of the most touching gifts I've ever received.

Clean her place for her.

Proclaim your love for her on a public billboard [*I've always wanted to do this with two common names that I made up, just to see what kind of acrimony I could induce into some strangers' relationship.*]

Obtain shots for a year for her pets like I did for Gracie and Beano. Nothing says, "I love you" quite like Heartworm pills.

Give her a facial. Her friends can tell you how to perform all the icky, useless procedures that she thinks makes her look better, but makes absolutely no difference to you.

Paint her a painting or write her a poem. Create something artistic that she inspires in you from wherever your strength and passion lies, even if it's a fish stick sculpture.

Buy her an occasional lottery ticket

Make her a coupon book redeemable for your services, such as cooking dinner or missing a football game on TV

> If she's a pack rat, get rid of some of her stuff for her. Giving her more gifts is one of the least romantic things you can do, because it compounds her clutter problem.

Rent her a "chick flick" and watch it with her. Suffer through it without flipping over to "The Man Show".

Hide a dozen small gifts around her place and make it a scavenger hunt

Mail her a pizza. You'd be surprised how fresh it stays
[*Unless you started with Dominoes to begin with*]

9. Miscellaneous

Nicknames

One of the most romantically endearing things you can do in a relationship is to coin a nickname for her. It's not always easy coming up with a nickname that's appropriate, endearing, original, personalized, and most importantly, embarrassing.

Names like Honey, Sweetie, and Baby are hackneyed clichés that say nothing about her individuality or your shared experiences. It does say a lot about your originality though. It says, "Hey! It doesn't matter who I'm dating, I can call her the same thing!"

I've dated a Flash, a Banana Wheel, a Legman, and a Squirmy, each with its own unique story. For instance, Banana Wheel came from a menu at Brigham's Ice Cream Shop. Some corporate marketing guru coined the term to help out the lackluster phrase "slice of banana".

You should continually be on the lookout for potential nicknames. A nickname won't always present itself, but always try to be aware if there's one in the making. Whatever you do, don't foist an inappropriate name upon her, just because a mind-numbing book like this tells you she should have one.

More importantly, don't give any of your body parts nicknames. For example, don't call your nose "El Schnozz". [*Dave breaks this rule and refers to his nose simply as "Tom".*] But if you do feel compelled to ignore this advice, especially don't name any of your body parts after her.

Romance Factor: Anywhere from Low to High.

Lesson: When ordering ice cream at Brigham's, you get way more banana in a Banana Spear than a Banana Wheel.

The Dancing Game

Ah...dancing. The beautiful transformation of music into motion. Many women consider dancing to be an indispensable element of romance. However, what you find is that as dancing partners, you soon fall into a repetitive rut in which you find out what works, and abandon trying difficult moves that tax your ability and your partner's feet.

In order to increase the diversity of your derring-do, consider the sincerest form of flattery. Next time you're out dancing, play the dancing game.

Subtly point to a couple and do your best to imitate them. [*Unless they start kissing. Eeeeuw, gross!*] That's it. This will not only prove to be challenging, but fun. The dancing game will help you increase your repertoire of moves and simultaneously combat the ennui that necessarily creeps into every couple's life. Just be prepared to feel a like dork [*Helpful tip: Enroll in Computer Science and then go to any party*], depending upon whom you're imitating.

If you tire of the game, you can play the Annoying Couple game by deliberately dancing too close to other couples. If you're slow dancing, you can augment this by taking on two distinct attitudes. For instance, you may have a dreamy, romantic expression, while your date may assume the "look around the room for help" mien.

If you feel self-consciousness about your dancing ability, the dancing game should quell your feeling once and for all when you realize how incredibly poorly most other people dance. You may be no better of course, but at least she'll see you're out there trying.

Dancing Paradox: Dancing is an awful lot like synchronized swimming, except there's no water and no one considers it romantic, although I can't for the life of me figure out why there is a difference.

Romance Factor: Moderate. It would be low, but you're still dancing after all, and that's romantic. And besides, if you end up just laughing, that's romantic too.

Lesson: Dancing falls under the greater concept of alternative forms of communication. Talking is probably the least romantic form of communication. Singing, writing, drawing and touch can potentially communicate far more to someone than your incessant yakking.

The Value of a Date

Back when I was in college, MIT held a semi-formal event at the Museum of Transportation [*The event should have been called "Nerds on Wheels"*] that allowed awkward geeks to spread their social wings by dancing and drinking cheap wine in front of old diesel engines. Tickets for the event were $10 per couple. I asked Liz to the event, because $10 seemed like a pretty good price for a semi-formal [*and incidentally, I liked her*].

What I didn't realize at the time was that couples had the option of taking a booze cruise up the Charles River, eventually docking across the street from the museum. The cruise cost $6. Throwing fiscal caution to the wind, I sprung for the extra $6. After all, every guy fancies himself as generous and fun loving [*Hint: They're not*] and I'm no exception!

But there were more hidden charges. The event planners chartered a bus to drive everyone back to campus after the event ended. The bus cost $.60 per person. The cost of the date had spiraled from $16 to $17.20. That's a 7.5% increase! I could have stalked 2 married women on the bus with the extra $1.20!

So that's where I had to draw the line. We were going to walk home. It was then that I realized that I knew exactly the value of this date.

Romance Factor: Low. Being parsimonious is romantic when buying your dream house together, not when you're on a date.

Lesson: It's good to know the value of your date. Just recognize that your date will probably also slap a value on you.

Getting There

When visiting a woman most guys consider one and only one transportation option—the automobile. Guys who do this miss out on a wonderful opportunity to be romantic, namely using self-propelled transportation to get there.

Why not consider running or bicycling there with a towel and a change of clothes? Bikemaster J.R. and I once showed up to a party after day 2 of a 3-day canoe odyssey. J.R. had a canoe-carrying device that allowed us to wheel the vessel a half-mile from the Charles River to the party. Jen, the hostess, was flabbergasted when she answered the door and saw us standing next to a canoe. Her reaction alone was worth the trip. Plus, for the entire party, we now had a great topic of conversation. [*The topic being Jen's wardrobe, not the canoe trip.*]

Romance Factor: Moderate to High.

Lesson: Athletic exertion is romantic. It demonstrates that you went through personal inconvenience and/or discomfort for her. Plus you can get a reasonable workout and simultaneously not pollute the planet. And the best part is, you can wear ratty clothes.

First Kiss

A word about kissing is in order. Your first kiss is one of the most dramatic opportunities you have to be romantic. Most men botch their first kiss terribly because they consider it a checkpoint on the way to a final destination.

A romantic man will savor the first kiss and try to make it special. But as much as you might savor it, do not underestimate a woman's ability to savor it even more. You want to make this moment as memorable as possible. And the more anticipation you build, the more memorable the kiss will be.

The best way to build anticipation is not to kiss her on the first date. Don't do it. Why would you? Are you so afraid that you'll never get another opportunity that you must kiss her ASAP? Or did you just get her all liquored up and she's ready?

If the feelings you are experiencing for her are real, they will be there the next time you see her. If they're not, then why are you kissing her in the first place? Don't answer that.

Once you've committed to forego the aforementioned osculation, you just might find that you become relaxed and can enjoy the date more. And you might also find out that she has other attractive qualities besides those pouty lips you're dreaming about.

And the best part is, not only will she realize that you see her more than just someone to slobber on, but when you actually do have that romantic first kiss, the anticipation will make it unforgettable.

Romance Factor: High.

Lesson: When Sharon asked me why I never kissed her, I replied that once you kiss someone, you can't unkiss them. Make sure that your level of physical intimacy never exceeds your level of emotional intimacy. [*Murray says, "If followed, this advice would drastically lower the amount of unhappiness in society."*] Most people guzzle intoxicants so they can ignore the part of their conscience that reminds them of this.

Homemade Greeting Cards

When six-year-old children want to express that they care about you, they have limited options in terms of ways to demonstrate it. They don't have a lot of buying power or mobility and probably don't have a lot of perspective on what you really want anyway.

But they do have time and creativity on their side and will often use these resources to show how they feel about you. So they make you something. They may make you a painting, a diorama, a sketch or greeting card. Now let me ask you. If a child gave you a store bought greeting card, how would that make you feel? Why would you feel any differently if an adult gets you a store bought greeting card?

Adults seem to have lost the ability to be creative. You can verify this the next time someone asks you what you want for your birthday. Respond with "I'd like you to do a 1 minute interpretive dance about our friendship" and you're guaranteed to get a greeting card.

Instead of purchasing your sentiment from a card factory, a romantic man like you might decide to make a card for the object of his affection. As long as it's from the heart, the card doesn't have to be fancy or witty or even rhyme. [*If you must rhyme, avoid meter problems and lame rhymes such as "happy" with "puppy" at all costs. Happy rhymes with sappy not puppy. Puppy makes you sound like a cretin.*]

If you're not artistic or very creative, you can cut pictures out of a magazine or the comics and put them together in some reasonably coherent fashion. Adding your own dialogue bubbles is a good idea.

For example, Akiko cut people's chins out of magazines and made me a collage that said, "Chins, Where would our faces end without them?" Todd once made a "Happy Secretaries Day" card for me. And Sherry sent Craig a clear postcard on which she wrote, "You are here."

Try it. She'll love the originality and time you spent thinking of her in a way that no one has thought of her before.

Romance Factor: High

Lesson: If you're looking for a word that rhymes with "Romance", try "Pants".

Lesson #2: For Valentine's day, don't feel compelled to rhyme anything with the word "Cupid". (Hats off to Art Hoctor, d. 1998.)

The Earring

I'm not really a big earring fan. I think it's silly to arbitrarily mutilate your body for the express purpose of adorning it with cheesy trinkets. But that doesn't mean women and smarmy Speedo-totin' European men don't like to wear earrings [*to match their handbags*].

One moonlit night in late 1987, I took Lacia to Sweylocken Park, a wooded park in the Seattle suburb of Bellevue. [*Motto: Hey, this is a good place for an industrial park.*] We spent the evening walking around the trails of the park and enjoying its quiet solitude.

We happened upon a gazebo built over a stream in the woods and rested. This was a perfect time to steal a few fairly innocent kisses. We lingered for a short time and then left.

When I dropped her off at her place, she became very upset when she realized she had lost one of her favorite earrings some time during the evening. She didn't really have a good idea of when she last had it.

But I had an inkling. I last remembered seeing them on her ears while in the Gazebo so I knew the general area of where the missing earring could be. I kept mum about the entire thing and went back to the park the next day. I walked directly to the Gazebo and looked around. I couldn't find the earring. If she lost it on the way back out of the park, it could be anywhere.

Just as I was about to give up, I saw it glinting in the streambed. I rescued the earring and brought it back to her, which was a really effective way of endearing her to me. [*What a mistake that turned out to be!!*]

Romance Factor: High.

Lesson: Go the extra mile to show her that you care. It helps not to have a real job to get the opportunity go to a park on a weekday.

Lesson #2: Before you get deeply involved in a relationship, check to make sure her bookcase isn't primarily comprised of self-help books.

The Earring, Part II

Twelve years later, while "Kissing for Food" [*This would be a great place for a hyperlink.*], Denise lost one of her favorite earrings. It seems that there's some correlation between kissing and losing earrings. Hmm.

As before, I decided to go back and look for the lost earring. Unbeknownst to Denise, I had appropriated her remaining earring so I'd know what I was looking for. The next day, I went back to the median strip and searched through the tall grass and road garbage. After combing through the area for a while, I found it!

Then I put the hubcap down and started searching for the earring, which, after about 20 minutes, I subsequently found as well.

Instead of just presenting it to her, I brought her take-out Chinese dinner and an orange. On the orange I had drawn a face and used her earrings as eyes. She was ecstatic because this was one of her favorite pairs.

Romance Factor: Still high, even 12 years later. It's just one of those timeless things, I guess.

Lesson: It's really difficult to draw anything on an orange because their rinds aren't porous. Bananas are much easier.

I'm Sorry

Inevitably, in any relationship you will do or say something for which you should apologize. Many men feel that the best way to apologize is by giving a woman a gift, such as flowers. Men who think that flowers can mend any transgression are shocked when they get:

While flowers may seem like a really sweet gesture, let's face it, all it shows is that you had 15 minutes and maybe $20. While this is certainly far better than not acknowledging or addressing your mistake at all, you're really just buying your way out of trouble.

A true apology is a far more difficult proposition. It consists of a healthy dose of remorse and more importantly, behavior modification. For if your behavior never changes, then how can you say you're truly sorry? You're not. You just want to be let off the hook. But of course, most guys don't think this way. They just want to say, "I'm sorry" or buy something and be left alone.

Understand that many women equate receiving a gift with repentance. But a woman of substantive character won't be fooled into forgiving disrespectful treatment with a trinket or flower. (Actually she will, but she shouldn't. Don't underestimate the power of a flower apology.)

One more word about flowers. When you give a woman flowers, it should always be in celebration of something positive. By all means buy her a flower when you're out picking up some groceries to show her that you thought about her.

But never give her flowers to make up for something negative, like an affront that requires an apology. If you only give flowers to say "I'm sorry", the message she gets is, "Every other day of the year, I'm not special enough to warrant flowers. But if I'm wronged, only then will I receive flowers to buy back my affection."

And while we're at it, don't ever buy her lingerie as a gift. It's a gift for you, not her. Besides, it's the woman who's sexy, not the clothes. You can put a negligee on a potato, but let's face it, when the negligee comes off, you're still with a potato. Conversely, a woman wearing a burlap sack, that takes care of her health and her figure, is far sexier than a french fry addict wearing a camisole. So my advice is skip the trip to Victoria's Secretion.

Romance Factor: High if you give her flowers on positive occasions. Low, if you give them to say, "I'm Sorry".

Lesson: If you don't want to alter your behavior, then you're probably not really sorry and shouldn't apologize for your actions at all. If you do, then not only are you not sorry, you're lying. And that makes you sorry in a completely different way.

Planting Cabbage

Liz and I had just started dating and I didn't feel I knew her well enough to give her flowers. At some point during one of our conversations, she lamented the state of her flowerbed.

She didn't have a lot of plants in it, and the ones growing there were not doing well. She mentioned a few of the species she might like to plant there, but the only thing I could remember was decorative cabbage.

So the next day I went to the nursery, got some cabbage plants, and planted them in her flower garden while she was at work.

She loved it. It's kind of ironic though. I didn't feel I knew her well enough to give her flowers, yet I felt that landscaping her yard was somehow appropriate.

Romance Factor: High.

Lesson: Long after your relationship has ended, she still has a lasting legacy of you in her yard that she has to pass by every day (hee hee!).

Markar K. Nahabidian

Back when I worked at DuPont [*Suggested Motto: Toxic chemicals for better living.*] in Billerica, MA, Dawn, Kim, and I took a business trip that had a layover in Dallas. Since I hadn't seen Tex in a long time, I called him and told him I'd be in town for a short layover. He said he'd meet me at the airport.

Now all of us at MIT were nerds, but even among us, we had our favorites. One of the guys we went to school with was named "Markar K. Nahabidian," a consummate geek with a mischievous streak. Because his name had an odd ring to us Anglicized students, we'd bandy it about on random occasions.

When I got off the plane, there stood Tex among the limo drivers with a big sign that read "Markar K. Nahabidian". Although I had no idea he'd have a sign, I hugged him without hesitation and exclaimed loudly, "I'm Markar K. Nahabidian"—not necessarily the easiest name to pronounce at first glance.

Dawn and Kim, who had no idea who Tex or Markar might be, did their best to distance themselves from me. But since we were traveling together on business for DuPont, [*Alternate Suggested Motto: Curing the cancers we cause*] they were compelled to stick closely by me. All the while, Tex accompanied us through the concourse, giving no indication that he was anything but a limo driver.

Eventually, we let them in on the joke, but the experience made me realize that this could give rise to a lot of romantic potential.

And so I have taken it upon myself to meet women at the gate posing as a limo driver, holding signs such as Legman or Squirmy, just to maximize embarrassment.

Romance Factor: Low, but fun.

Lesson: If you really miss someone while they're away, chances are you've thought about them a lot. Making a sign is a way of demonstrating that you've missed them. It shows that you gave thought to her arrival and take delight in it, rather than it being an onerous chore done out of obligation.

Caveat: It's bad form to greet her in this fashion if you actually do drive a limo for a living.

Pizza Guy

Four times a year, Denise works market. This means she spends the entire weekend at the Apparel Mart, representing clothing lines to buyers from stores large and small. The frenetic pace of market is such that she not only misses lunch, but often can't even place or take phone calls.

I thought it might be romantic to bring her and her co-workers some food to sate their hunger. However, the entrance fee to the Apparel Mart is prohibitive. I had to find another way to enter the market without incurring the onerous fee.

So the night before, I went to a pizza place and obtained a pizza box. The next morning, I dressed up as a pizza delivery guy [*For authenticity's sake, I wore a dorky hat, but fortunately, I don't have acne.*] and went to the bagel shop. I bought some fresh hot bagels and cream cheese and put them in the box. Then I went to the Apparel Mart.

It was more difficult to break their ultra-high security net than I imagined. They wouldn't let me through registration without paying the hefty entrance fee. But I was not to be denied.

I went around to the service entrance in the back. Once they saw the dorky hat and pizza box, they waved me right through. And so Denise and her co-workers all ate bagels that morning.

Romance Factor: High.

Lesson: This experience underscores the importance of publicly acknowledging your feelings for her. It works on the same principle as sending her flowers at the office. She will love the fact that everyone envies her, even if they think she's dating a pizza delivery guy.

10.
Five Guys
You'll Always
Lose Out To

THIS BOOK HAS BEEN DEDICATED TO showing you by example how to be more romantic. However it has never been unequivocally established that being romantic is the most desirable course of action in a relationship.

Even if you were to follow all the advice in this book to the letter, you are guaranteed of nothing. [*See legal department or Tex for implied warranty*] There is still a multitude of guys that will attract far more women than you ever will. And given the opportunity, many women will choose these guys over you every time.

The Fast Car Guy

Fact: Fast Car Guys attract women. While some guys might own performance cars because fine engineering is their passion, Fast Car Guys mostly care about their image and will buy their fast car whether or not they can afford it. They will often get their fast car for the specific purpose of getting women to go out with them.

This means that their whole mindset is one of perniciously trying to dupe a woman into believing in their false image of prosperity. Fast Car Guys are selling their image, not their personality, romance, or integrity, because hey, go with your strengths. And what are their strengths? A fast car. That's it! Their entire identity is their car.

And while it's enjoyable to go cruising around in a red Porsche, it's difficult to believe that some women will base entire relationships on it. But they will [*Translation: My self-esteem is so low, that someone else's car makes me feel good about myself*]. And the confounding thing is that you will always lose out to this guy, unless you happen to be…

The Rich Guy

The Rich Guy already has a fast car. And not only can he can afford it, he can afford other toys. That's why you'll always lose out to a rich guy.

Even though you occasionally see romantic films where the good-hearted average income guy gets the beautiful girl instead of the evil rich guy, it doesn't work that way in real life. All poor-to-middle class guys have some faults and no rich guys are completely evil. [*Except Bill Gates*]

And anyway, that's the movies. Remember, most filmmakers became filmmakers so that people would watch the fantasies of grandeur they developed when they hung out in the AV room in high school with all the other dateless geeks, brooding over the injustice of it all.

The thing that most women never realize about rich guys is that because they're rich, women are expendable—merely a commodity that can be bought, traded, or sold [*on eBay*].

Rich Guys don't have to pay attention to women. They have their secretaries pay attention to them because Rich Guys are too busy, well, getting rich. So if a Rich Guy starts missing too many of his woman's birthdays or anniversaries, you can bet he'll be getting a new secretary soon. [*Unless he's dating her on the side.*]

It doesn't matter though. Many women prefer money to romance. That's just the way it is. So a Rich Guy will be chosen over you every time, unless you happen to be...

The Actor

The first thing you should know about "The Actor" is that Acting is a profession in which success is measured by how well you fool people into believing that you're someone you're not. Given that, it's incomprehensible how easy it is to lose out to an Actor.

Like Rich Guys, Actors have nice cars and money. Plus they're famous, are often good looking, and go to high-tone parties with fascinating Hollywood luminaries like Darva Conger.

Women go absolutely wild over The Actor [*And rock stars. Mustn't forget rock stars*]. I think the reason is societal. Instead of boring you with sociological rubric, let me bore you with this instead. If you made a list of people you didn't actually know (but knew their names) most would be actors.

And women want to be around them. Even third-tier stand-up comedians are given consideration over you because the mystique of the stage and the long shot of "making it big" is more enticing than being with someone who actually cares about you, like a Romantic Guy.

But even actors can lose out to…

The Italian Guy

I just don't understand what's so inherently romantic about Italian Guys. [*And to a lesser extent, other sweaty Europeans.*] Women visit Italy in droves for the express purpose of getting leered at by slimeballs when they could be getting leered at by slimeballs here at home.

For some reason, there is something about the way Italian Guys leer that makes women melt. Maybe it's the accent. Maybe it's the implied flattery in everything they say. Or maybe they're just not as picky about wooing corpulent women.

Whatever it is, you can bet that women don't sit around fantasizing about meeting a Bulgarian Guy or a Nigerian Guy or a Pakistani Guy. You'll never hear a woman say, "Korean men are so romantic." Nope, it's always an Italian. That's why you'll always lose out to an Italian Guy. [*Unless you're looking for an Italian woman. They won't get anywhere near Italian guys. However, Italian women seem to be the only women in the world who are drawn to Jewish guys.*]

For instance, consider the way a Romantic Guy might say goodnight on a date.

Romantic Guy: *Before saying goodnight, may I please place my tongue in your mouth just once?*

Now let's face it, while his delivery and wording are awful, what RG is proposing is really not all that uncommon on a date. Plus he's trying to be polite by asking. But you can bet that a woman will rebuff him at all costs and tell her friends about the disgusting pig that she dated last night.

Now consider an Italian Guy's smooth pitch (Imagine him taking her hand, looking deeply into her eyes and saying this with an Italian Accent):

Mi Amoré. You are such a beautiful lady. Please do me the wonderful honor of allowing me, my cousin Hermano, and his pack of llamas to come to your apartment for a night of passionate romance. Neither my wife nor my mistresses will mind.

Most women will jump at this opportunity to disrespect themselves. It all sounds so romantic when said with an Italian accent.

And even though it won't seem quite so romantic the next day when cleaning up after the llamas, these women will forever think wistfully back to their evening of romance with the Italian Guy(s). Italian Guys gets chosen over Romantic Guys every time. There's just no explaining it. But the most baffling to me is...

The Bad Boy

The Bad Boy is the Kingpin. He will beat every other guy without fail. You know him. Very aloof and distant. He'll never communicate. He may have a ponytail, definitely has a piercing, drives a motorcycle and has tattoos [*Hey, look how rebellious I am! I wouldn't think twice about engraving graffiti on my body! But don't you dare ding my motorcycle!*]. He'll never call and can never be pleased. You can't tame him. He's a challenge.

There is not a romantic bone in his body, but every woman wants him. The Bad Boy fills a woman's pathological need to change her man. No better challenge exists. Not to mention that dating him makes her a "bad girl" [*to be neglected and mistreated*].

Although a few more enlightened women outgrow the Bad Boy, many women make them a lifestyle. They'll fervently throw themselves at him with their entire beings, trying desperately to get his attention. They will do things for him that no self-respecting woman would do for anyone else, particularly a Romantic Guy who treats her with respect. And they're happy getting nothing in return, except the satisfaction of landing the Bad Boy. Of course, you can never really land a Bad Boy.

So when the Bad Boy inevitably dumps the woman, she is completely surprised by the experience. She really thought she was the one who was going to change him. Needless to say, she wasn't. He goes on with his life completely unconcerned, with a gaggle of other women bidding for his walled off emotions.

Of course, she will pine away for him as no other, remembering just how sweet it was to occasionally have the attention of a jerk who neglected her most of the time. And the worst part is, the pain she suffered at his hands is turned upon the next Romantic Guy she meets who ends up paying for all his transgressions that she jumped at the chance to be subject to.

Lesson: Because he dominates all 5 categories, Robert DeNiro has to be the most desirable man on the planet

Conclusion

OK ROMANTIC GUYS, here's the formula for being a romantic man in easy-to-digest USA Today format.

~ *Components of Romance* ~

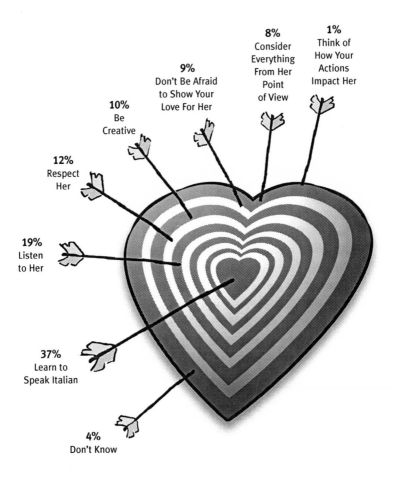

8%
Consider
Everything
From Her
Point
of View

1%
Think of
How Your
Actions
Impact Her

9%
Don't Be Afraid
to Show Your
Love For Her

10%
Be
Creative

12%
Respect
Her

19%
Listen
to Her

37%
Learn to
Speak Italian

4%
Don't Know

That's just about it! If you just did some of this stuff occasionally, you'd be amazed at how romantic women will consider you. Plus, you'll be amazed at how much more of a loving harmonious relationship you could have. And finally, you'll be amazed at how much more SportsCenter you could watch without having her complain.

Zusammenfassung

My parents raised me to respect all people [*Even Telemarketers*], but especially women. I've done my best to honor women and treat them with dignity. I've always assumed that women want to be treated with dignity and respect.

However, my life experiences indicate that guys don't treat women very well, and many accept this treatment as a matter of course. This wouldn't be so objectionable to me if I hadn't repeatedly been passed over for these other guys for most of my life.

Was it the Kung-Fu drop kick? Or was it my not-so-smooth line at the drive-thru? Maybe I failed to spend that extra sixty cents at a semi-formal.

The cabal of golden boys with shallow qualities will always be treated well by women. These guys get chosen because of the product they're selling, be it their sporty Camaro, the cigar they're smoking, their stinky European shoes or the sunglasses they feel is imperative to wear at night.

I hope that as a result of this book, some women, somewhere, will realize that romantic guys are best. Don't settle for a guy just because his pitch is polished, he looks like an Adonis or he tries to cloud your judgement by plying you with alcohol at an ear piercing dance club. [*Although given the way some men treat women, this would be a nice change.*]

You deserve better.

Take the time to find out if he's romantic.

Is This Book Fiction?

The names and places used in this book are all real. I have written entire chapters about people I barely knew and have completely excluded others who are or have been very dear to me.

At times you have seen names repeated in the book that may refer to two different people. Occasionally, a single person has been referred to by two or more different names. And sometimes names have been changed [*I'd make a lousy census taker*].

Although I've tried to describe the experiences as accurately as possible, I have taken a few liberties with the stories when memory has failed me or when it was expedient. But every event happened more or less as I've described.

Thanks for reading my tiny book.

About the Author:

STEVE SILBERBERG graduated from M.I.T. in 1984 with both Bachelor and Master of Science degrees in Electrical Engineering and Computer Science. Steve is President of an Internet Lost and Found site called ELFsearch.com. He also runs Callipygian AdVentures, a weight-loss backpacking outfitting service. Steve has been a software contractor for over 19 years serving dozens of clients including DuPont, Polaroid, Tektronix, Acadian Asset Management, and Data I/O. Steve's other careers include College Professor, Aerobics Instructor, Museum Curator, Expert Witness, Stand-Up Comedian, and Filmmaker. Steve's Air Sickness Bag Museum has garnered international press and national prime-time TV and radio coverage.

Steve hates people and prefers to spend his time backpacking in the wilderness. [*But he likes writing about himself in the 3rd person like a self-important putz.*]

NOTES:

If I write in this book, the resale
value on half.com will drop significantly.

Printed in the United States
200043BV00007B/160-210/A